HEALTHY AND HAPPY

Family and Friends

Louise Spilsbury

First published in 2010 by Wayland
Copyright © Wayland 2010

Wayland, 338 Euston Road, London NW1 3BH
Wayland, Level 17/207 Kent Street, Sydney, NSW 2000

British Library Cataloguing in Publication Data
Spilsbury, Louise.
    Family and friends. — (Healthy and happy)
    1. Families—Juvenile literature. 2. Friendship—Juvenile
    literature.
    I. Title II. Series
    306.8'5-dc22

ISBN 978-0-7502-6105-0

Produced for Wayland by Calcium
Design: Paul Myerscough and Geoff Ward
Editor: Sarah Eason
Editor for Wayland: Joyce Bentley
Illustrations: Geoff Ward
Picture research: Maria Joannou
Consultant: Sue Beck, MSc, BSc

Printed in China

Pic credits: Fotolia: Jerome Berquez 6; Istockphoto: Digitalskillet 22, Mark Evans 16, 18, Rosemarie
Gearhart 26, Sheryl Griffin 2, 10, Kim Gunkel 23, Bonnie Jacobs 13, Cat London 21, Ekaterina
Monakhova 25, Neustockimages 8, Muammer Mujdat Uzel 24; Shutterstock: Elena Kouptsova-Vasic
17, Rob Marmion 7, Monkey Business Images 1, 4, 9, 15, 19, 20, Losevsky Pavel 12, Margot
Petrowski 27, Lesley Rigg 11r, Jane September 11l, 14, Harald Høiland Tjøstheim 5.

Cover photograph: Shutterstock/Rob Marmion

Wayland is a division of Hachette Children's Books, an Hachette UK company.

www.hachette.co.uk

Contents

Family and friends

Family and friends are special. They care about us and we care about them. They are people that we can turn to for help and **advice**.

Different relationships

Most people have many different **relationships**. You may have friends in your school or your street. There are different kinds of families, too. Some have two parents, others have one. Some children are **adopted** and others may live with a relative.

Friends are people we can share both happy and sad times with.

For most people around the world, family and friends are the most important things in their lives.

Same feelings

People live in many different ways and in many different places. One thing that is the same for everyone is that family and friends are important to us. To be healthy and happy, we all need people who care about us!

Families

A family is made up of children and the adults who care for them. Families should care for each other. How do they do this?

Family support

The adults in families give children somewhere to live, food to eat and clothes to wear. They also teach you how to behave. We share everyday times with our family, such as washing the dishes. We also share special times with them, like birthdays or going on holiday.

Families have fun, but they also work together.

Family rules

Adults in a family make rules. These rules are there to keep you healthy and happy. As you get older, you may want to change some of the rules. Try to talk about this with your family in a friendly way. Remember, they only want the best for you.

HEALTHY HINTS

If you are unhappy at home or if you feel your family are unkind to you, try talking to a teacher or another adult you trust.

Different relatives make up your family, including aunts, uncles and grandparents.

Friendships

Being a good friend and having good friends is an important part of keeping happy and healthy. Do you know what makes a good friend?

Good friends

Good friends care about each other. They try to understand each other's feelings and moods. Good friends are happy for each other to have other friends. They trust each other to be **loyal**.

Some friends like the same things as you, but other friends may like different things.

You can be best friends with more than one person.

Friendship problems

Friends can encourage you to try new things that are fun. Sometimes, a friend may try to **persuade** you to do something you do not want to do or that you know is wrong. This is not being a good friend. Friends can disagree without hurting each other's feelings, so say no to your friend and explain why.

HEALTHY HINTS

Try to make new friends wherever you go. Friends can make you happy and you will get something different from each new friendship.

Caring for each other

Family and friends show they care for each other in different ways. How do you show someone they are special to you?

Showing you care

There are lots of different ways to show you care. You can show you care with the things you say. You could ask your dad how he feels if he has been ill. You could tell a friend what you like about them. Showing you care makes people feel happy.

Giving someone in your family a hug is a way of showing that you care about them.

Showing feelings

You can also show how you feel without words. Our faces let people see our feelings. People smile to show they are happy and frown to show they are cross or worried. The way we behave shows our feelings, too. A parent might show they care by giving you a kiss or a hug.

What feelings do you think these faces show?

It's a fact!

You use more face **muscles** to frown than to smile, so it is easier to smile!

Teamwork

A team is a group of friends or family who work together to get something done. What makes a good team?

Working together

People often work together when they have a job to do. Classmates work together to finish a project. A football team works together to score goals. To do the job well, teams share out different roles. That way everyone on the team does a fair share of the work.

Together, a team of people can do things that one person could not do alone.

It can feel great to be part of a team!

Making teams work

To make teams work, people share **decisions**. People in a team do what most of the team members want to do. You may be asked to do something you don't want to do, like play a new position in a football game. But it may work out better for the team in the end.

HEALTHY HINTS

Many teams wear a uniform or t-shirts with their team name or logo. This helps members spot each other in a crowd and it makes people feel that they are part of a team.

Give and take

Part of being in a family and having friends is give and take. It means sharing and helping each other. How do you give and take?

Taking turns

It is important to take turns in a game or wait for your turn to speak in class. Friends take turns to help each other, too. For example, a friend might help you practise lines for a play. Then you take your turn and help them practise for a sports match or game.

When your parents make time to do fun things with you, such as swimming, think about what you could do for them in return.

Sharing chores

There is a lot to do in a home, so families share **chores**. Children may take care of family pets, empty the bins or do some cleaning. While you may not like the idea of chores, most people find that helping others makes them feel good!

HEALTHY HINTS

You sometimes have to do chores that you don't like. Why not offer to do a job that you do like? That way you will get to do a chore you like and your family will be happy that you offered to help!

To make your family happy, you need to make time for your chores as well as for play.

Talking together

Family and friends need time to talk. Talking together is a chance to share thoughts, secrets and news. It also makes people feel close.

Speaking

When you are chatting with someone, try not to **interrupt** them. Wait for them to finish talking before you speak. Say what you think, but respect other people's ideas, too. It is also good to ask questions – especially if you don't understand something.

This girl is putting her hand up to ask her teacher a question.

16

The way people behave or move their hands when they talk helps you to understand what they are saying.

Listening

When you listen carefully, you find out more. A good listener hears what people say and concentrates on what the other person is saying, rather than thinking about what they will say next. When you listen well, you will also understand what the other person is feeling.

17

Sorting out problems

It is normal for friends and families to argue sometimes. After all, we all have our own **opinions**. It is important to know how to talk about them.

How to argue

When you disagree with someone, it is okay to say so. Try to say you disagree in a friendly way, and be polite. Do not shout or say mean things. Talk calmly and quietly. Try to see the other person's point of view, even if you do not agree with them.

If someone is shouting at you, try not to shout back. Instead walk away and tell them you will be happy to talk when they have calmed down.

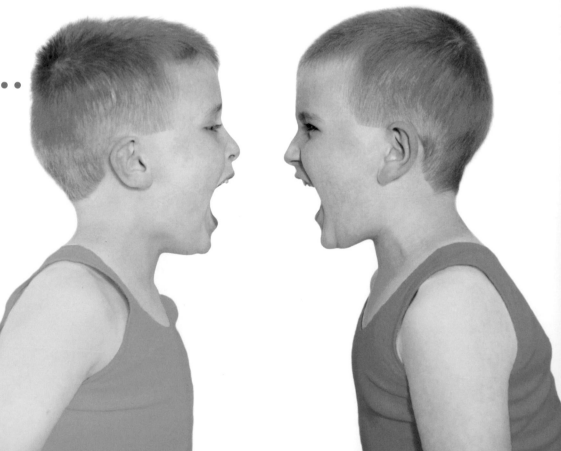

When you don't agree with someone, say so in a friendly way. That way, there will be no bad feelings afterwards.

Sort it out

If you fall out with someone, the best thing to do is talk about it. Try to choose somewhere quiet to talk, away from other people. Before talking, think about what happened. Did you say or do something you could say sorry for? Saying sorry when you really mean it usually helps.

HEALTHY HINTS

When you feel really angry and want to shout, try going into another room. Take time out or count to 10 until you feel calm again.

Being kind

The things we do and say affect our family and friends. When people are kind to each other, everyone feels happier.

How to be kind

Being kind means trying to understand how other people feel. Before you say something, think how you would feel if someone said it to you. It is good to tell people the things you like about them or the things they do well. There is no need to tell them the things you do not like about them!

Being mean to someone can make them feel sad, angry and lonely.

Bullying

Bullying is when someone is very unkind to another person. A bully calls people names, hurts them or makes them feel left out. If you see someone being bullied, try to help them. Helping others makes us feel good, too.

If you see someone sitting alone, the kind thing to do is to go and talk to them.

It's a fact!

Tell your parent or teacher if you are being bullied. They will be able to help you to sort things out.

Respecting differences

The world is made up of many different kinds of people. All of us have the **right** to be happy and to be treated fairly.

Differences

People like different foods and different games. They have different-coloured eyes and hair. Some people speak or dress differently and some wear glasses or use a wheelchair. What people are like on the inside is more important than how they look.

It is fun to be friends with boys and girls and people who are older and younger than us, too.

Showing respect

It is unfair to make fun of someone who is different from you, or to avoid playing with them. People feel unhappy when they are left out or treated unfairly. The world would be a boring place if we were all the same. Knowing different people is far more fun!

We show people respect by being polite and kind to them.

HEALTHY HINTS

Try to get to know people who are different from you. The best friendships are often with people who seem different from us at first!

23

When you lose someone

It is very hard to lose someone you care about. What happens when a friend moves to another school, a parent leaves home or a pet dies?

Feelings

When someone leaves or dies, we miss them. It will help to talk about that person and your feelings with other people. Or you could write down how you feel in a letter, diary or notebook.

When you first lose a friend or family member, you may feel sad, angry and afraid.

Moving on

It is healthy to spend some time thinking about your loss, but it is unhealthy to do it all the time. You need to make time to do things that make you happy. Have a day out doing something fun. Find ways to make friends. You could join a club or take up a new sport.

HEALTHY HINTS

If you or a friend moves house, you can still keep in touch by phone, email or writing.

Finding new things to do is a good way to cope with loss.

Who can help?

People feel unhappy when they have problems with people they care about. Who can help if things are going wrong with family or friends?

Help for friends

If you stop being friends with someone and cannot sort it out, ask for help. Ask a parent, teacher or older student to talk with you both. They can listen to what has happened and help you work things out.

Worrying about stuff is bad for you. Get help when you need it, so you can stay healthy and happy!

About 2,500 children
call ChildLine every day.
Most children call about
bullying or problems
in their family.

*Talking to someone
about a problem
can make it better.*

Family troubles

Children need a family that cares for them and
does not hurt them. If you are having problems
at home, talk to a teacher or other adult you
trust. Or you could call a helpline telephone
number like ChildLine. Some families go to a
family therapist. This is someone who helps
families to work out their problems.

Make a friendship bracelet

You will need:
- embroidery thread, wool or cord in three different colours
- scissors
- sticky tape

Why not show a friend you care by making them a friendship bracelet!

1. Cut two long pieces from each coloured thread.

2. Hold all six threads at one end, with the pairs of coloured thread together.

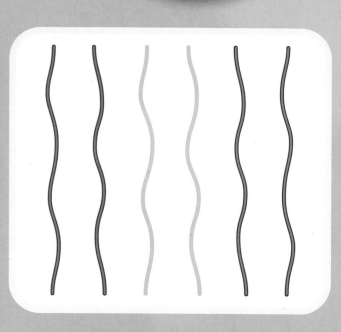

3. Tie a knot at one end of the six threads. Use sticky tape to stick this knotted end onto a table.

4. Separate the threads into the three pairs of colours and lay them flat.

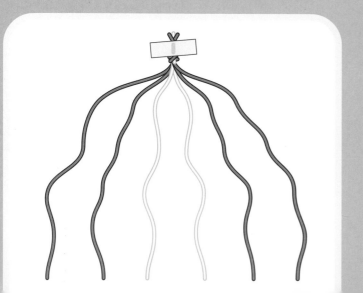

5. Plait the three pairs of threads together. To do this, take the pair of threads on the right and cross it over the middle pair of threads. Now do the same with the pair of threads on the left. Keep crossing the right and then the left pair of threads over and pull the plait tight each time.

6. When you think the bracelet is long enough to go round your friend's wrist, tie a knot in the other end and remove the sticky tape.

7. Now the bracelet is ready for your friend to wear!

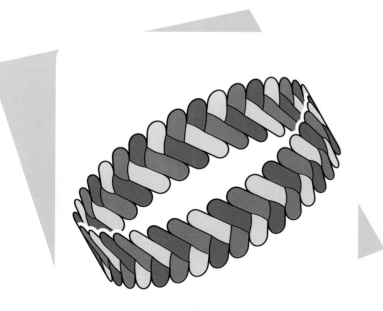

Family and friends topic web

Use this topic web to discover themes and ideas in subjects that are related to family and friends.

PSHE
- Understanding that healthy relationships are good for us and keep us well.
- Understanding that unhealthy relationships are bad for us.
- How to be a good friend.
- How to show your feelings.
- How to listen to other people's feelings.
- Taking responsibility for the way in which you treat other people.
- Draw your own family tree.

GEOGRAPHY
- Understanding that family and friends are important to people everywhere.
- Understanding that friends can come from many different places and many different cultures.

FAMILY AND FRIENDS

ART AND DESIGN
- How to design and make a friendship bracelet from coloured thread or fabric.

SCIENCE
- Understanding that some children have biological or birth parents and other children have adopted parents.

Glossary

adopted when a child is part of a family they were not born into
advice suggestion about what someone should do or say
chores jobs, such as housework or gardening
decisions choices made after thinking or talking about the best thing to do
family therapist someone who is trained to help families with problems
interrupt to stop someone else from speaking
loyal being faithful to someone and always supporting them
muscles parts of the body that make other body parts move
opinions feelings, thoughts and ideas about something
persuade to make someone do something by telling them they should
relationships connections between people
right something that everyone should have by law or because it is fair

Find out more

Books
Keeping Healthy: Relationships by Carol Ballard (Wayland, 2007)

Health Choices: Relationships by Cath Senker (Wayland, 2007)

Websites
If you are having relationship problems, you can get advice and help from the ChildLine Website at:
http://www.ChildLine.org.uk

Index